Reflections on the Life of the Spirit

Ruhi Institute

Books in the Series:

Below are the current titles in the series designed by the Ruhi Institute. The books are intended to be used as the main sequence of courses of a formal educational program for youth and adults aimed at building capacity for service. The Ruhi Institute is also developing a set of courses that branch out from the third book in the series for training Bahá'í children's classes teachers, and this is indicated in the list as well. It should be noted that the list will undergo change as experience in the field advances, and new titles will be added as an increasing number of curricular elements under development reach the stage where they can be made widely available.

Copyright © 1987, 1994, 1999, 2007 by the Ruhi Foundation, Colombia
All rights reserved. Edition 1.1.1 published September 1994
Edition 3.1.1 March 2007
ISBN 978-1-890101-59-6

Palabra Publications
7369 Westport Place
West Palm Beach, Florida 33413
U.S.A.
1-561-697-9823
1-561-697-9815 (fax)
books@palabrapublications.info
www.palabrapublications.info

Contents

TO THE COLLABORATORS

The Ruhi Institute uses the term "collaborator" to refer to all who study, teach, or apply its courses, wherever they may reside. These participants are indeed collaborators, because all share the Institute's purpose: to use the courses as means of serving the Cause and promoting the well-being of humanity. In every study group there is always a more experienced person who acts as a tutor. The other members of the group constitute the "students" who seek the tutor's help with their studies. However, it is clearly understood by all participants that they are engaged in a reciprocal process, one in which everyone learns. The responsibility of learning rests with each participant. It is the student who undertakes the active work of learning. The tutor facilitates this process, and also gains new insights into the material. The relationship is not that of a learned one with a group of ignorant people.

"Understanding the Bahá'í Writings", "Prayer", and "Life and Death" are often the first units that a group of collaborators chooses for its studies. We hope the tutor will carefully go over the ideas presented here. Those who are studying these units for the first time need not concern themselves with this introduction as they will have to analyze it at a later time, when they themselves will act as tutors of this book for other groups of beginners.

In studying the courses of the Ruhi Institute, participants are expected to achieve three levels of comprehension. The first is a basic understanding of the meaning of words and sentences of passages from the Writings, which constitute the core of these courses. Thus, for example, after reading the quotation, "The betterment of the world can be accomplished through pure and goodly deeds, through commendable and seemly conduct", the student is asked, "How can the betterment of the world be accomplished?" At first glance, this type of question may appear too simple. But the following two observations from actual experience point to some of the reasons for the adoption of a simple approach to this basic level of understanding.

Often for the study of the first unit in the book, the tutor will divide the group into pairs; one person in each pair is asked to read the quotation aloud, and the other is asked to formulate a question, the answer to which would be the quotation. For some, such an exercise is extremely easy and is carried out swiftly. Others find constructing a question from a sentence challenging at the beginning and need practice before they acquire the necessary skills. This type of exercise is not, of course, applicable to most of the units of the Ruhi Institute and is done less and less frequently as the students advance in their studies.

The second observation has to do with the participants who insist on giving their own opinions and strongly resist repeating the quotation as the answer to a question. Clearly, there is nothing wrong in having and expressing one's own ideas; but an understanding of the Writings must begin by focusing the mind on what is being read before allowing one's imagination to roam and personal opinions to flow freely. It is quite likely that by first developing in the believers, early in their study of the Faith, a capacity to focus attention on the immediate and explicit meaning of sentences they read from the Holy Writings, we will be contributing to the creation of unity of thought in our communities, since such a unity can only be attained when personal opinions are illuminated by Divine Wisdom.

It is important to note here that achieving this first level of comprehension never involves a long discussion on the meaning of single words outside the context of the material being studied. In fact, most tutors find that using a dictionary to help the participants understand difficult words actually interferes with their learning. It seems far more useful to help them learn how to infer the meanings of words through discussion of whole phrases and paragraphs.

The second level of comprehension is concerned with applying some of the concepts in the quotations to one's daily life. For example, exercise number one in the second section of the unit "Understanding the Bahá'í Writings", which asks the participant to identify certain types of conduct as commendable, is easy to answer; yet it requires the group to think about some of the obvious applications of the corresponding quotation in the lesson. However, not all the exercises of this level can receive immediate and obvious answers. For instance, to decide whether the statement "There are so few good people in the world that their actions do not have any effect" is true or false, the students have to establish how this statement contradicts the corresponding quotations they have studied from the Writings of Bahá'u'lláh.

The third level of understanding requires the participants to think about the implications of the quotations for situations with no apparent or immediate connection with the theme of the quotation. For example, the question of whether Bahá'ís may confess their sins to others refers to the prohibition against confession as a means of absolving sin, a deeply-rooted practice of Catholicism. The tutor should present this prohibition as the group consults on the implications of the verse, "Bring thyself to account each day ere thou art summoned to a reckoning."

Many years of experience with the courses of the Ruhi Institute have shown that examining ideas at these three levels of understanding helps collaborators create the conscious basis of a life of service to the Cause. But what may surprise someone who is unfamiliar with this experience is that efforts to prolong consultation on each idea beyond these levels, by introducing too many related concepts, actually diminish to a great extent the effectiveness of the courses. This is partly because each course should establish a rhythm of progress, so that students will have a distinct sense that they are advancing rapidly according to their own capacities. This does not mean that lessons should be passed over quickly and superficially without careful analysis of the exercises. Groups that have taken this superficial approach, merely filling in answers, have never lasted beyond a few sessions. The point to remember is that once an idea is understood and some insights into its applications have been gained, the group should advance to the next point in the lesson. Another reason for the caution against prolonged discussions has to do with the habit of speculation that unfortunately develops in some of our communities from time to time. It is natural that a verse from the Writings should bring to mind myriads of noble and beautiful ideas. To share these ideas with the friends on appropriate occasions conduces to joy and happiness. But care must be taken so that this practice does not become an exercise in the expression of ego and an insistence on the sovereignty of personal opinion. The experience of the Ruhi Institute has shown that we do not suppress the imagination or the personality of the participants when we refrain from posing questions such as, "What does this mean to you?"; on the contrary, we are helping to nurture the development of communities which look first to the Writings as the principal basis of consultation whenever they are faced with a question. We believe that the habit of thinking about the implications of the Writings with the minimum of personal interpretation would eliminate a great share of the disagreements which afflict consultation in many communities and would make the activities of our communities more effective.

In preparing to teach the three units of this book, the tutor would do well to examine each section, categorize the exercises according to the three levels of comprehension and, if necessary, think of additional exercises that will stimulate consultation about each concept.

The purpose of the first unit of the book, "Understanding the Bahá'í Writings", is to develop in the participants the habit of reading the Writings and thinking about them, beginning at first with one-sentence statements. To read the Holy Writings every day, at least in the morning and at night, is one of the very important ordinances of our Faith. But reading the Writings is not the same as reading the thousands of pages that a literate person sees during a lifetime. To read the Sacred Word is to drink from the ocean of Divine Revelation. It leads to true spiritual understanding and generates forces that are necessary for the progress of the soul. In order to reach true understanding, however, one must think deeply about the meaning of each statement and its applications in one's own life and in the life of society.

"Prayer" is the second unit included in this book. In preparing to teach the unit, the tutor needs to reflect on its three principal objectives. The first is to clarify the concept of prayer itself and to help the participants understand its great importance as one of the laws of this Dispensation. In order to achieve this objective, it is sometimes necessary to dissipate doubts and carefully examine ideas that may have their roots in erroneous interpretations of the past. Above all, this objective implies clear understanding of the necessity to observe this law, a need that is no less essential than that of nourishing our bodies every day.

Beyond observing the law of prayer, each person must feel a profound desire to pray. Therefore, the second objective of this course is to awaken in participants the desire to "converse with God" and to feel the joy of being near to Him. Moreover, from an early age, everyone should develop spiritual habits; the habit of praying daily is among the most important of these.

The third objective of the course concerns the attitudes with which prayer should be approached. Unfortunately, humanity is steadily losing its understanding of how to pray, substituting empty and meaningless rituals for indispensable inner conditions. Therefore, the study groups should consult a great deal on the sections of the unit which refer to the attitudes of heart and mind that help one enter the state of prayer and to the conditions that should be created in one's surroundings at the time of prayer.

The third unit of the book, "Life and Death", is a special challenge for the collaborators of the Ruhi Institute when they study it for the first time and also, later, when as tutors they help others learn its content. The theme of life and death has been included in the first book of the Institute's program because it is considered essential for the participants' understanding of the paths of service they will choose to follow. Service in this world has to be understood in the fullest context of life which extends beyond our earthly existence and continues forever as our souls progress through the worlds of God. In a process of education, in contrast to the mere acquisition of simple skills, it is essential that participants become increasingly conscious of the meaning and significance of what they are doing. As this consciousness emerges, students come to see themselves as active, responsible "owners" of their learning, and not as passive recipients of information given to them by their teachers.

Each section of this unit opens with a thematic statement or quotation from the Bahá'í Writings and continues with a series of exercises designed to help participants comprehend the language and the concepts of the statement. Unlike the other two units which include exercises to help participants think about the application of ideas in their own lives and their communities, here, owing to the abstract nature of the material, all the exercises operate at the conceptual level. Only in the last section are participants asked to reflect on the implications of the course for their lives.

As mentioned before, participants in the Ruhi Institute courses should be encouraged to avoid unnecessary speculation and to be content with concrete answers that can be deduced directly from the statements. Yet, a few of the exercises contain questions that cannot be answered quickly or in a clear-cut way. These questions are designed to raise awareness about the subject; if participants merely think about such questions, the objective of learning will be fulfilled.

It should also be mentioned that the language of the quotations presented in this unit is more difficult than that of the other two units. The tutor must be very careful not to give too much attention to difficult words, but to ensure that participants understand the central idea of each quotation, which is precisely what the exercises try to bring out.

In order for good results to be achieved from the study of this unit, it is essential to avoid introducing too many ideas into a single session. Above all, it is important to follow the sequence of ideas as presented:

1. How life begins, and what is death.

    * The soul is a spiritual entity, created by God.

    * The soul and the body, together, constitute the human being.

    * Death is just a change of condition; afterward, the soul progresses eternally.

2. The purpose of our lives.

    * The purpose of life is to know God and to attain His presence.

    * One who recognizes the Manifestation draws near to God, and one who rejects Him condemns himself to a life of misery and remoteness from God.

    * Just as in the womb of the mother one acquires the powers needed for this world, so in this world should we acquire the powers needed for the next world.

3. The nature of the soul.

    * The soul is a sign of God.

    * A soul which is faithful to God will reflect His light and be drawn to Him.

- Worldly attachments and vain desires impede the soul's flight towards God and finally make it weak and impotent.

- God has bestowed on man the capacity to reflect all His names and attributes.

4. The need for the Manifestation of God as the Universal Educator.

  - The capacities of the human being are latent; they can only be developed with the help of the Manifestation of God.

  - To know the Manifestation of God is to know God.

  - Through spiritual education, the treasures hidden within us can be revealed.

5. The condition of the soul after death.

  - The faithful soul will attain a sublime position and happiness, but the unfaithful soul will recognize its loss and be consumed in remorse.

  - No one knows his own end; therefore, we should forgive others and not feel superior towards them.

  - In the next world, the holy souls become acquainted with all mysteries and behold the beauty of God.

  - In the next world, we will recognize our loved ones and enjoy companionship with the friends of God; we will remember the life we had in this material world.

6. The appropriate attitude towards the present conditions of our lives.

  - Nothing should sadden us in this world, because days of blissful joy await us.

Understanding the Bahá'í Writings

Purpose

To develop the capacity to read the Bahá'í Writings
and to meditate on their meaning in order to fulfill
the obligation of studying the Writings every day.

Practice

Read daily, in the morning and evening,
some of the Writings of the Faith.

SECTION 1

In this unit you will study short passages from the Writings of the Faith and think about how you can apply them to your life. You will begin at the simplest level, by reading a one-sentence statement from the Writings and then responding to a question, the answer to which is the statement itself. For the purpose of this exercise, it will be useful for you to study the sentence with the aid of another participant in the course. In that case, one of you would pose the question and the other reply. You would then change roles. This type of exercise is not one that you will repeat throughout the courses of the Ruhi Institute, although, in the future, there might be passages that lend themselves to the use of this technique. While simple, the exercise will help you to reflect on the meaning of passages and to memorize them.

"The betterment of the world can be accomplished through pure and goodly deeds, through commendable and seemly conduct." [1]

1.	How can the betterment of the world be accomplished? _____

_____ _____

"Beware, O people of Bahá, lest ye walk in the ways of them whose words differ from their deeds." [2]

2.	In whose ways should we not walk? _____

_____

"O Son of Being! Bring thyself to account each day ere thou art summoned to a reckoning . . ." [3]

3.	What should we do before we are summoned to a reckoning? _____

_____

"Say: O brethren! Let deeds, not words, be your adorning." [4]

4.	What should be our true adorning? _____

_____

"Holy words and pure and goodly deeds ascend unto the heaven of celestial glory." [5]

5.	What do holy words and pure and goodly deeds do? _____

_____

SECTION 2

Below are a number of exercises related to the quotations you have just studied. Some of the questions are easy to answer, and it is not worthwhile to spend too much time discussing them. When the exercise is challenging, however, you should pause and, with the help of your tutor, explore it thoroughly.

1. "Commendable" means something that merits praise. Which of the following are commendable?

   a. To be a good worker? _____

   b. To respect others? _____

   c. To be studious? _____

   d. To be a liar? _____

   e. To be lazy? _____

   f. To help others progress? _____

2. What does the phrase "ere thou art summoned to a reckoning" mean? _____
   _____

3. Decide whether the following statements are true or false:

   a. There are so few good people in the world that their actions do not have any effect. T ☐ F ☐

   b. Something is correct when it is in agreement with the opinions of other people. T ☐ F ☐

   c. Something is correct when it is in agreement with the teachings of God. T ☐ F ☐

4. The following are pure and goodly deeds:

   a. Teaching the Faith. T ☐ F ☐

   b. Stealing. T ☐ F ☐

   c. Taking care of and teaching children. T ☐ F ☐

   d. Praying for the progress of others. T ☐ F ☐

   e. Telling a small lie to get out of trouble. T ☐ F ☐

   f. Helping others and expecting a reward. T ☐ F ☐

5. The following actions are in agreement with the words of a Bahá'í:

   a. Having an alcoholic drink. T ☐ F ☐

   b. Being kind. T ☐ F ☐

c. Treating everyone equally.   T ☐   F ☐

d. Having sexual relations outside of marriage.   T ☐   F ☐

6. Is it permissible for a Bahá'í to confess to another person? _____

7. What should we do instead of confessing? _____

_____

8. What does "the heaven of celestial glory" mean? _____

_____

9. What is the effect of bad deeds on the world? _____

_____

10. What effect do bad deeds have on those who commit them? _____

_____

SECTION 3

In this section you are again asked to study quotations from the Writings. Note that for some passages it is possible to formulate more than one question. But this should not be overdone; do not try to think of every question possible.

"Truthfulness is the foundation of all human virtues." [6]

1. What is the foundation of all human virtues? _____

"Without truthfulness progress and success, in all the worlds of God, are impossible for any soul." [7]

2. What is impossible without truthfulness? _____

_____

"Beautify your tongues, O people, with truthfulness, and adorn your souls with the ornament of honesty." [8]

3. With what should we beautify our tongues? _____

4. With what should we adorn our souls? _____

_____

"Let your eye be chaste, your hand faithful, your tongue truthful and your heart enlightened." [9]

5.   How should our eye be? _____ Our hand? _____

     Our tongue? _____ Our heart? _____

"They who dwell within the tabernacle of God, and are established upon the seats of everlasting glory, will refuse, though they be dying of hunger, to stretch their hands and seize unlawfully the property of their neighbor, however vile and worthless he may be." [10]

6.   What would a Bahá'í refuse to do even if he were dying of hunger? _____

     _____

     _____

SECTION 4

As you probably noticed in Section 2, some of the exercises require precise answers. In such cases, if there is doubt about the answer, your tutor will be able to help you arrive at the desired conclusion. For other exercises, it is the discussion itself that is valuable, and the tutor may accept various answers from the participants. In the following, question number 4, while complex, is of the first kind, and question number 6 of the second.

1.   Truthfulness is the foundation of all human virtues. List five virtues. _____

     _____

     _____

2.   Can we acquire these virtues without truthfulness? _____

3.   Decide whether the following statements are true or false:

     a.   A person can be just, even if he tells lies.   T ☐   F ☐

     b.   Someone who steals has a faithful hand.   T ☐   F ☐

     c.   A faithful hand never touches what does not belong
          to it.   T ☐   F ☐

     d.   To read pornographic books and magazines is con-
          trary to Bahá'u'lláh's counsel to have an eye that is
          chaste.   T ☐   F ☐

     e.   Truthfulness means not lying.   T ☐   F ☐

     f.   Honesty is an ornament of the soul.   T ☐   F ☐

g. A person who is not truthful can progress spiritually. T ☐ F ☐

h. It is all right to tell lies now and then. T ☐ F ☐

i. Stealing is acceptable before God, if one is hungry. T ☐ F ☐

j. To take something without permission from its owner, thinking that we will return it later, is not stealing. T ☐ F ☐

k. If a friend has a tree with a lot of fruit on it, taking some without asking permission is all right. T ☐ F ☐

l. When we act honestly and are fair and truthful, our heart is enlightened. T ☐ F ☐

4. Is it possible to lie to oneself? _____

5. What do we lose when we tell a lie? _____
   _____

6. What would the world be like if we were all truthful and honest? _____
   _____
   _____
   _____

SECTION 5

Study the following quotations and try to learn them by heart. Memorizing quotations from the Writings is highly rewarding, and you should make every effort to do so. Yet there are some people who, for various reasons, find memorization almost impossible. If you happen to have such a difficulty, then you should try to learn the quotations so well that you can express the ideas with words as close to the original text as possible.

"A kindly tongue is the lodestone of the hearts of men. It is the bread of the spirit, it clotheth the words with meaning, it is the fountain of the light of wisdom and understanding. . . ." [11]

1. How can a kindly tongue be described? _____
   _____
   _____

2. What effect does a kindly tongue have on words? _____
   _____

"O ye beloved of the Lord! In this sacred Dispensation, conflict and contention are in no wise permitted. Every aggressor deprives himself of God's grace." [12]

3. According to this quotation, what is not permitted in this Dispensation? _____

    _____

4. What does the aggressor do to himself? _____

    _____

"Nothing whatever can, in this Day, inflict a greater harm upon this Cause than dissension and strife, contention, estrangement and apathy, among the loved ones of God." [13]

5. What conditions inflict the greatest harm to the Cause of God? _____

    _____

    _____

"Do not be content with showing friendship in words alone, let your heart burn with loving-kindness for all who may cross your path." [14]

6. What type of friendship should not satisfy us? _____

7. What should burn brightly in our heart? _____

    _____

"When a thought of war comes, oppose it by a stronger thought of peace. A thought of hatred must be destroyed by a more powerful thought of love." [15]

8. What should oppose a thought of war? _____

    _____

9. What should destroy a thought of hate? _____

    _____

SECTION 6

Carry out the following exercises:

1. "Lodestone" is another word for magnet. In what way does a kindly tongue act

    like a lodestone? _____

2. Decide whether the following phrases proceed from a kindly tongue:

   a. "Don't bother me!"   Yes ☐ No ☐

   b. "Why don't you understand this?"   Yes ☐ No ☐

   c. "Would you care to wait, please?"   Yes ☐ No ☐

   d. "What terrible children!"   Yes ☐ No ☐

   e. "Thank you, you're very kind."   Yes ☐ No ☐

   f. "I don't have any time now. I'm busy."   Yes ☐ No ☐

3. Decide whether or not the following situations present conflict:

   a. Two people express different opinions during Bahá'í consultation.   Yes ☐ No ☐

   b. Someone does not go to a Bahá'í meeting because he is not on speaking terms with the owner of the house.   Yes ☐ No ☐

   c. Some of those who are staying at the Bahá'í Institute during a course constantly complain that the others are not doing their duties.   Yes ☐ No ☐

   d. Two Bahá'í teachers cannot agree on where they want to go on a teaching trip.   Yes ☐ No ☐

4. Decide whether or not the following represent estrangement and apathy:

   a. A friend arrives at the Bahá'í Institute and no one greets him warmly.   Yes ☐ No ☐

   b. At the Bahá'í Institute, the students divide themselves into small groups, and each group keeps to itself.   Yes ☐ No ☐

   c. At the Institute, during study hours, everyone is studying and not talking.   Yes ☐ No ☐

   d. Two teachers, although they do not fight, refuse to go out teaching together.   Yes ☐ No ☐

5. Decide whether the following phrases are true or false:

   a. One should say exactly what one thinks of others; it does not matter if their hearts are offended.   T ☐ F ☐

   b. It is all right to tell lies to avoid conflict.   T ☐ F ☐

   c. Conflict can be overcome with love and kindness.   T ☐ F ☐

   d. Words are more effective when they are said with love.   T ☐ F ☐

   e. It is all right to fight with someone if he starts it.   T ☐ F ☐

f. One has the right to be sharp with others when one is sick or sad.   T ☐   F ☐

g. It is not kind to laugh at others when they do something wrong.   T ☐   F ☐

h. Mentioning the faults of others is all right because it is not backbiting.   T ☐   F ☐

i. When hard feelings exist between friends, each one should make a special effort to become closer to the other.   T ☐   F ☐

j. When hard feelings exist between friends, each one should wait until the other makes an effort to move closer.   T ☐   F ☐

SECTION 7

Study the quotations below and memorize them:

". . . backbiting quencheth the light of the heart, and extinguisheth the life of the soul." [16]

"Breathe not the sins of others so long as thou art thyself a sinner." [17]

"Speak no evil, that thou mayest not hear it spoken unto thee, and magnify not the faults of others that thine own faults may not appear great . . ." [18]

"O Son of Being! How couldst thou forget thine own faults and busy thyself with the faults of others? Whoso doeth this is accursed of Me." [19]

1. What effect does backbiting have on the one who backbites? _____

    _____

2. What should we be aware of before thinking about other people's sins? _____

    _____

3. What will happen to us if we magnify the faults of others? _____

    _____

4. What should we remember when we think of other people's faults? _____

    _____

SECTION 8

Carry out the following exercises:

1. What happens to the progress of the soul of a person who focuses on other people's faults? _____

2. What effect does backbiting have on the Bahá'í community? _____
    _____

3. What do you do when a friend starts to talk about another person's faults? _____
    _____

4. Decide whether the following statements are true or false:

    a. If we talk about someone's real faults, we are not backbiting.   T ☐   F ☐

    b. If we talk about a person's good qualities and his faults at the same time we are not backbiting.   T ☐   F ☐

    c. Backbiting has become a custom in our society, and we should develop the discipline to avoid it.   T ☐   F ☐

    d. If the listener promises not to repeat what we say about another person, there is no harm in backbiting.   T ☐   F ☐

    e. Backbiting is one of the greatest enemies of unity.   T ☐   F ☐

    f. If we acquire the habit of talking about other people all the time, we are in danger of falling into backbiting.   T ☐   F ☐

    g. When the capacities of different people are discussed in a Local Spiritual Assembly meeting in order to assign certain tasks, this is backbiting.   T ☐   F ☐

    h. When we feel the urge to backbite, we should think about our own faults.   T ☐   F ☐

    i. When we know a person is doing something which harms the Faith or the community, we should discuss it with the rest of the Bahá'ís.   T ☐   F ☐

    j. When we know of someone who is doing something that harms the Faith or the community, we should only inform the Local Spiritual Assembly.   T ☐   F ☐

k. It is not wrong for a married couple to talk about other people's faults since they should not have secrets from each other.   T ☐   F ☐

The course you have just completed has a very special purpose. Bahá'u'lláh teaches that each person should read from the Holy Writings every morning and every evening. During this course, you have already begun to form this habit which is extremely important for your spiritual progress. Now you may wish to acquire a book of the Writings of Bahá'u'lláh and read parts of it every day. *The Hidden Words* is a good first choice.

REFERENCES

1. Bahá'u'lláh, cited in Shoghi Effendi, *The Advent of Divine Justice* (Wilmette: Bahá'í Publishing Trust, 1990), pp. 24-25.

2. *Gleanings from the Writings of Bahá'u'lláh* (Wilmette: Bahá'í Publishing Trust, 1994), CXXXIX, p. 305.

3. Bahá'u'lláh, *The Hidden Words* (Wilmette: Bahá'í Publishing Trust, 1994), Arabic no. 31, p. 11.

4. Ibid., Persian no. 5, p. 24.

5. Ibid., Persian no. 69, p. 46.

6. 'Abdu'l-Bahá, cited in *The Advent of Divine Justice,* p. 26.

7. Ibid., p. 26.

8. *Gleanings from the Writings of Bahá'u'lláh,* CXXXVI, p. 297.

9. *Tablets of Bahá'u'lláh Revealed after the Kitáb-i-Aqdas* (Wilmette: Bahá'í Publishing Trust, 1997), p. 138.

10. *Gleanings from the Writings of Bahá'u'lláh,* CXXXVII, pp. 298-99.

11. Ibid., CXXXII, p. 289.

12. *Will and Testament of 'Abdu'l-Bahá* (Wilmette: Bahá'í Publishing Trust, 1991), p. 13.

13. *Gleanings from the Writings of Bahá'u'lláh,* V, p. 9.

14. *Paris Talks: Addresses Given by 'Abdu'l-Bahá in Paris in 1911-1912* (London: Bahá'í Publishing Trust, 1995), p. 2.

15. Ibid., p. 19.

16. *Gleanings from the Writings of Bahá'u'lláh,* CXXV, p. 265.

17. *The Hidden Words,* Arabic no. 27, p. 10.

18. Ibid., Persian no. 44, p. 37.

19. Ibid., Arabic no. 26, p. 10.

Prayer

Purpose

To understand the importance of daily prayer and
to develop the required attitudes of prayer.
To memorize five prayers and
understand their meaning.

Practice

Visit at least two Bahá'ís and
study a prayer with them.

SECTION 1

'Abdu'l-Bahá tells us that prayer is "conversation with God". "To converse" means to talk with someone; thus, when we are praying we are talking with God.

If a person truly loves another, his most fervent desire is to be in his loved one's presence and to converse with him. Our prayer should be a loving conversation with our Creator, the One True God. During prayer, we who are weak can beseech and supplicate God and ask for His assistance. We should always keep in mind that prayer in its purest state serves to bring us nearer to God and helps us attain the Divine Presence.

After studying the preceding two paragraphs, answer the following questions:

1. What is prayer? _____

2. What is the most fervent desire of a person who loves another? _____
    _____

3. How, then, should our conversation with God be? _____
    _____
    _____

4. What do the words "beseech" and "supplicate" mean? _____
    _____

5. Is the purpose of prayer only to ask for what we need? _____
    _____

6. What are the most important effects of prayer? _____
    _____
    _____

7. Who is 'Abdu'l-Bahá? _____
    _____

SECTION 2

Muḥammad has said that prayer is like a ladder suspended between heaven and earth by which we can ascend to paradise.

In the Long Obligatory Prayer, Bahá'u'lláh has revealed: **"I beseech Thee . . . to make of my prayer a fire that will burn away the veils which have shut me out from Thy beauty, and a light that will lead me unto the ocean of Thy Presence. "** [1]

1. Who is Muḥammad? _____

2. What does Muḥammad say about prayer? _____
_____
_____

3. In what sense is prayer like a ladder? _____
_____

4. Mention some veils that shut us out from God. _____
_____
_____
_____

5. Can prayer be like a fire? What does it consume? _____
_____

6. Can prayer be like a light? Where does it lead us? _____
_____

7. Can you write four phrases on the nature of prayer?
   a. Prayer is _____
   b. Prayer is _____
   c. Prayer is _____
   d. Prayer is _____

SECTION 3

Study the following words of 'Abdu'l-Bahá and meditate on them:

> **"There is nothing sweeter in the world of existence than prayer. Man must live in a state of prayer. The most blessed condition is the condition of prayer and supplication. Prayer is conversation with God. The greatest attainment or the sweetest state is none other than conversation with God. It creates spirituality, creates mindfulness and celestial feelings, begets new attractions of the Kingdom and engenders the susceptibilities of the higher intelligence."** [2]

1. What is the sweetest state in the world of existence? _____
_____

2. What does "state of prayer" mean? _____

3.   Mention some of the conditions created by prayer. _____

_____

_____

_____

SECTION 4

Study the following words of Bahá'u'lláh and meditate on them:

> "Intone, O My servant, the verses of God that have been received by thee, as intoned by them who have drawn nigh unto Him, that the sweetness of thy melody may kindle thine own soul, and attract the hearts of all men. Whoso reciteth, in the privacy of his chamber, the verses revealed by God, the scattering angels of the Almighty shall scatter abroad the fragrance of the words uttered by his mouth, and shall cause the heart of every righteous man to throb. Though he may, at first, remain unaware of its effect, yet the virtue of the grace vouchsafed unto him must needs sooner or later exercise its influence upon his soul. Thus have the mysteries of the Revelation of God been decreed by virtue of the Will of Him Who is the Source of power and wisdom." [3]

1.   What does "intone" mean? _____

_____

2.   How should we intone the verses of God? _____

_____

_____

_____

3.   What effect will the sweetness of our melody have on our own souls? _____

_____

_____

4.   What effect will the sweetness of our melody have on the hearts of all men? __

_____

5.   What does "recite" mean? _____

_____

6.   What does "scatter" mean? _____

_____

7. What effect can our prayers have on others who do not even know that we are praying? _____

_____

_____

_____

_____

_____

SECTION 5

We know that God created us. He is the All-Knowing, the All-Wise. He knows what we want and what we need. Then why should we pray? God does not need our prayers; nevertheless, the progress of our souls depends on prayer, because prayer is the food of the soul. When we pray we are taking in spiritual nourishment. Through the bonds of love connecting us to the divine worlds, we receive the blessings of God. Prayer increases our capacity to enjoy spiritual gifts and to experience true happiness.

The pathway to God is straight and narrow. Innumerable obstacles may block our way. By means of ardent, sincere and constant supplication, we can overcome the obstacles and be guided along this path. Prayer helps us to advance towards God and not lose sight of our special destiny. This is why we should pray constantly that through the love of God our souls may develop and be strengthened, and that we may firmly walk the path of eternal happiness with steadfastness. 'Abdu'l-Bahá says:

> **"In the highest prayer, men pray only for the love of God, not because they fear Him or hell, or hope for bounty or heaven. . . . When a man falls in love with a human being, it is impossible for him to keep from mentioning the name of his beloved. How much more difficult is it to keep from mentioning the Name of God when one has come to love Him. . . . The spiritual man finds no delight in anything save in commemoration of God."** [4]

> **"If one friend loves another, is it not natural that he should wish to say so? Though he knows that that friend is aware of his love, does he still not wish to tell him of it? . . . It is true that God knows the wishes of all hearts; but the impulse to pray is a natural one, springing from man's love to God."** [5]

1. Why should we pray? _____

_____

_____

2.   Complete the following sentences:

In the _____ prayer, men _____ only for _____
of God, not because they fear Him or _____, or hope for _____
or heaven. When a _____ falls _____ with a human being,
it is _____ for him to keep from mentioning the _____
of his _____. How much more _____ is it
to keep from _____ the Name of _____ when one
has come to _____ Him. The spiritual man finds no _____ in
anything save in _____ of God.

SECTION 6

Memorize the following passages from the Long Obligatory Prayer revealed by Bahá'u'lláh:

"O God, my God! Look not upon my hopes and my doings, nay rather look upon Thy will that hath encompassed the heavens and the earth. By Thy Most Great Name, O Thou Lord of all nations! I have desired only what Thou didst desire, and love only what Thou dost love." [6]

"Make my prayer, O my Lord, a fountain of living waters whereby I may live as long as Thy sovereignty endureth, and may make mention of Thee in every world of Thy worlds." [7]

"Too high art Thou for the praise of those who are nigh unto Thee to ascend unto the heaven of Thy nearness, or for the birds of the hearts of them who are devoted to Thee to attain to the door of Thy gate. I testify that Thou hast been sanctified above all attributes and holy above all names. No God is there but Thee, the Most Exalted, the All-Glorious." [8]

SECTION 7

When we pray we should center our thoughts on God. We should forget the things of the world, what is going on around us, and even our own selves. Bahá'u'lláh says:

"O Son of Light! Forget all save Me and commune with My spirit. This is of the essence of My command, therefore turn unto it." [9]

To forget all save God is not easy. Effort is needed. It requires great yearning. When our hearts are pure and free of our own imaginings and desires, our prayers have their greatest effect.

"Depend thou upon God. Forsake thine own will and cling to His, set aside thine own desires and lay hold of His . . . " [10]

Imagine a glass of pure, sweet milk. We can derive various products from this milk, such as butter, cheese, and cream. But if we add a drop of poison, that milk is contaminated and its usefulness is lost. It is no longer pure. We cannot use it for anything. The poison that man puts into his life is his ego. We should free ourselves of ego if we want our prayers to have great effect.

Another very important requirement for reaching the true state of prayer is faith. We should have complete trust in the mercy of God and be certain that He will grant what is best for us. 'Abdu'l-Bahá says:

"Spirit has influence; prayer has spiritual effect. Therefore, we pray, 'O God! Heal this sick one!' Perchance God will answer. Does it matter who prays? God will answer the prayer of every servant if that prayer is urgent. His mercy is vast, illimitable. He answers the prayers of all His servants. He answers the prayer of this plant. The plant prays potentially, 'O God! Send me rain!' God answers the prayer, and the plant grows. God will answer anyone." [11]

1. What should be our attitude when we pray? _____

    _____

2. Where should our thoughts be centered when we pray? _____

    _____

3. How can we forget all save God? _____

    _____

    _____

4. What effects do our prayers have when our hearts are pure and free of vain imaginings and selfish desires? _____

    _____

5. Mention some of the spiritual qualities we can ask for in our prayers. _____

    _____

    _____

6. Explain why it is important to pray with faith. _____

    _____

    _____

7. What is meant by "the mercy of God"? _____

    _____

8.   What happens when we say our prayers but our minds are occupied with other things?

_____

SECTION 8

In preceding sections we have learned about the nature of prayer, how to pray, and why we should pray. It is important to understand that prayer is a law of Bahá'u'lláh and should be obeyed. Not only should we pray every day, but also recite the Words of God, at least every morning and evening. Bahá'u'lláh says:

> **"Recite ye the verses of God every morn and eventide. Whoso faileth to recite them hath not been faithful to the Covenant of God and His Testament, and whoso turneth away from these holy verses in this Day is of those who throughout eternity have turned away from God. Fear ye God, O My servants, one and all."** [12]

The prayers which we recite in the morning, at night or at other times can be chosen from the many prayers revealed by the Báb, Bahá'u'lláh and 'Abdu'l-Bahá. The time we spend praying and the number of prayers we say depend on our needs and our spiritual thirst. However, Bahá'u'lláh has revealed three daily obligatory prayers. Shoghi Effendi says:

> **"The daily obligatory prayers are three in number. The shortest one consists of a single verse which has to be recited once in every twenty-four hours at midday. The medium (prayer) has to be recited three times a day, in the morning, at noon, and in the evening. The long prayer which is the most elaborate of the three has to be recited once in every twenty-four hours, and at any time one feels inclined to do so.**

> **"The believer is entirely free to choose any one of those three prayers, but is under the obligation of reciting either one of them, and in accordance with any specific directions with which they may be accompanied.**

> **"These daily obligatory prayers, together with a few other specific ones, such as the Healing Prayer, the Tablet of Aḥmad, have been invested by Bahá'u'lláh with a special potency and significance, and should therefore be accepted as such and be recited by the believers with unquestioning faith and confidence, that through them they may enter into a much closer communion with God, and identify themselves more fully with His laws and precepts."** [13]

1.   As Bahá'ís, do we pray only when we need something? _____

2.   Why do we obey the laws of Bahá'u'lláh? _____

_____

3.   At least how many times should we pray each day? _____

4. What are we doing by not reciting the verses of God in the morning and at night?

_____

5. What does "turn away" mean? _____

6. How many daily obligatory prayers has Bahá'u'lláh revealed? _____

_____

7. Should we recite all three prayers every day? _____

8. If we choose to say the Long Obligatory Prayer, how many times should we say it each day? _____

9. How many times, if we choose to say the Medium Obligatory Prayer? _____

10. How many times, if we choose the Short Obligatory Prayer? _____

11. Mention some of the prayers which have a special power. _____

_____

_____

12. Recite the Short Obligatory Prayer.

13. To what do you testify in this prayer? _____

_____

_____

14. What does the word "obligatory" mean? _____

_____

SECTION 9

We have learned that Bahá'u'lláh has made prayer a law for this age and that when we pray and recite the verses of God we are being faithful to His Covenant. We also know that Bahá'u'lláh has given us prayers for all occasions and that He Himself has invested some of them with special power. Among them are the obligatory prayers. These obligatory prayers are said when we are alone, communing with God. The other prayers can be said alone or when we are with other people. We should keep in mind that congregational prayer where an obligatory prayer is recited in a group according to a certain ritual does not exist in the Bahá'í Faith. The Prayer for the Dead is the only congregational prayer prescribed by Bahá'í law. It is to be recited by one of those present while the remainder of the group stands in silence.

When we pray we center our thoughts and our innermost being on God. We should wait awhile before beginning to pray to try to cleanse our minds of the things of this world. To achieve this end, some people silently repeat to themselves the Greatest Name. When we finish reciting prayers, we should reflect on the words we have just read and not move abruptly into another activity. This practice is the same whether we are praying alone or with other people. When another person is praying we can feel as though we are praying ourselves. We should listen closely to the words the other is saying and maintain a prayerful attitude.

1. To what are we being faithful when we pray every day? _____

2. What kinds of prayers did Bahá'u'lláh reveal? _____
   _____

3. How many obligatory prayers are there? _____

4. Can we recite the obligatory prayers in meetings? _____

5. What should we do before praying? _____
   _____

6. What do we do at the end of a prayer? _____
   _____

7. What attitude should we have when, in a meeting, another person is praying?
   _____

8. What should we be thinking about when another person is praying in a meeting?
   _____

9. Is it right to be looking in the prayer book for what we will read while another person is praying? _____

10. Write a description of the respectful attitude we should show when we pray, especially in meetings. _____
    _____
    _____
    _____
    _____
    _____

REFERENCES

1. Bahá'u'lláh, *Bahá'í Prayers: A Selection of Prayers Revealed by Bahá'u'lláh, the Báb, and 'Abdu'l-Bahá* (Wilmette: Bahá'í Publishing Trust, 1993), p. 8.

2. Words of 'Abdu'l-Bahá cited in *Star of the West,* vol. VIII, no. 4 (17 May 1917), p. 41.

3. *Gleanings from the Writings of Bahá'u'lláh* (Wilmette: Bahá'í Publishing Trust, 1994), CXXXVI, p. 295.

4. 'Abdu'l-Bahá, cited in *Spiritual Foundations: Prayer, Meditation and the Devotional Attitude,* comp. the Research Department of the Universal House of Justice (Wilmette: Bahá'í Publishing Trust, 1980), no. 35, p. 12.

5. Ibid., no. 34, p. 12.

6. Bahá'u'lláh, *Bahá'í Prayers*, pp. 8-9.

7. Ibid., p. 9.

8. Ibid., p. 12.

9. Bahá'u'lláh, *The Hidden Words* (Wilmette: Bahá'í Publishing Trust, 1994), Arabic no. 16, p. 8.

10. *Selections from the Writings of 'Abdu'l-Bahá* (Wilmette: Bahá'í Publishing Trust, 1997), no. 38, p. 85.

11. *The Promulgation of Universal Peace: Talks Delivered by 'Abdu'l-Bahá during His Visit to the United States and Canada in 1912* (Wilmette: Bahá'í Publishing Trust, 1995), p. 246.

12. Bahá'u'lláh, *The Kitáb-i-Aqdas: The Most Holy Book* (Wilmette: Bahá'í Publishing Trust, 1993), p. 73.

13. Shoghi Effendi, *Principles of Bahá'í Administration* (London: Bahá'í Publishing Trust, 1973), p. 7.

Life and Death

Purpose

To understand that life is not the changes and
chances of this world, and its true significance
is found in the development of the soul.
True life, the life of the soul, occurs in this world
for a brief time and continues eternally
in other worlds of God.

SECTION 1

The soul has its origin in the spiritual worlds of God. It is exalted above matter and the physical world. The individual has his beginning when the soul associates itself with the embryo at the time of conception. But this association is not material; the soul does not enter or leave the body and does not occupy physical space. The soul does not belong to the material world, and its association with the body is similar to that of a light with a mirror which reflects it. The light which appears in the mirror is not inside it; it comes from an external source. Similarly, the soul is not inside the body; there is a special relationship between it and the body, and together they form a human being.

1. Decide whether the following statements are true or false according to the preceding paragraph:

   a. The soul has its origin in the spiritual worlds of God. T ☐ F ☐

   b. The individual has his beginning when the soul associates itself with the embryo. T ☐ F ☐

   c. The soul belongs to the material world. T ☐ F ☐

   d. The soul is within the body. T ☐ F ☐

   e. The soul and body together make up a human being. T ☐ F ☐

   f. The soul is exalted above the physical world. T ☐ F ☐

   g. The relationship that exists between the soul and the body is like that of a light and the mirror which reflects it. T ☐ F ☐

2. This paragraph implies:

   a. True life begins when the individual is born into this world. T ☐ F ☐

   b. Material existence continues in the other worlds of God. T ☐ F ☐

   c. The body is the owner of the soul. T ☐ F ☐

   d. Life consists of the things that happen to us every day. T ☐ F ☐

3. Questions:

   a. Where does the soul originate? _____
   _____

   b. When does an individual have his beginning?_____
   _____
   _____

   c. What makes up a human being?_____
   _____

d. What worlds does the soul belong to? _____

_____

SECTION 2

There is a very special relationship between the soul and the body, which together form a human being. This relationship lasts only the span of a mortal life. When this ceases, each one returns to its origin, the body to the world of dust and the soul to the spiritual worlds of God. Having emanated from the spiritual realms, created in the image and likeness of God, and capable of acquiring divine qualities and heavenly attributes, the soul, after its separation from the body, progresses for all of eternity.

1. Questions:

a. How long does the relationship between the soul and the body last? _____

_____

b. Where does the body go after death? _____

c. Where does the soul go after death? _____

_____

d. How long does the soul progress? _____

e. Which is more important, the soul or the body? _____

_____

f. Where does the soul come from? _____

g. What part of man was created in the image and likeness of God? _____

_____

h. How does our life change when we die? _____

_____

i. When does life end? _____

j. What happens to the relationship between the body and the soul when we die?

_____

_____

2. The paragraph says or implies that:

a. Death is a punishment.   T ☐   F ☐

b. Our bodies were made in the image and likeness of
    God.   T ☐   F ☐

c. The relationship between the body and soul only lasts
    the span of a mortal life.   T ☐   F ☐

d. The body is capable of acquiring divine attributes.   T ☐   F ☐

e. The soul will progress forever.   T ☐   F ☐

f. Death is the end of life.   T ☐   F ☐

g. After being dead, our bodies will rise up.   T ☐   F ☐

h. At death, our soul has more freedom than it had in
    this world.   T ☐   F ☐

i. Life ends with death.   T ☐   F ☐

j. We should fear death.   T ☐   F ☐

SECTION 3

Bahá'u'lláh says:

> **"And now concerning thy question regarding the soul of man and its survival
> after death. Know thou of a truth that the soul, after its separation from the
> body, will continue to progress until it attaineth the presence of God, in a state
> and condition which neither the revolution of ages and centuries, nor the
> changes and chances of this world, can alter. It will endure as long as the
> Kingdom of God, His sovereignty, His dominion and power will endure. It
> will manifest the signs of God and His attributes, and will reveal His loving-
> kindness and bounty."** [1]

1.   Questions:

a. What is the separation of the soul and the body called? _____

b. How long will the soul continue to progress? _____
    _____

c. What are the attributes and signs that the soul will manifest in the other world?
    _____
    _____
    _____

d. What will it reveal? _____

e. Does the soul continue living after death? _____

2. The above words of Bahá'u'lláh imply that:

    a. The soul will attain the presence of God.   T ☐ F ☐

    b. The soul's condition will be affected by the changes of this world, even after death.   T ☐ F ☐

    c. The Kingdom of God will last forever.   T ☐ F ☐

    d. The soul has the capacity to manifest the attributes of God, like loving-kindness and generosity.   T ☐ F ☐

    e. The state of the soul after death is more exalted than its state in this world.   T ☐ F ☐

SECTION 4

Bahá'u'lláh says:

> "Know thou that every hearing ear, if kept pure and undefiled, must, at all times and from every direction, hearken to the voice that uttereth these holy words: 'Verily, we are God's, and to Him shall we return.' The mysteries of man's physical death and of his return have not been divulged, and still remain unread. By the righteousness of God! Were they to be revealed, they would evoke such fear and sorrow that some would perish, while others would be so filled with gladness as to wish for death, and beseech, with unceasing longing, the one true God—exalted be His glory—to hasten their end.

> "Death proffereth unto every confident believer the cup that is life indeed. It bestoweth joy, and is the bearer of gladness. It conferreth the gift of everlasting life.

> "As to those that have tasted of the fruit of man's earthly existence, which is the recognition of the one true God, exalted be His glory, their life hereafter is such as We are unable to describe. The knowledge thereof is with God, alone, the Lord of all worlds." [2]

1. Mark true or false:

    a. The soul of man comes from God and will return to Him.   T ☐ F ☐

    b. Man's physical death is a mystery.   T ☐ F ☐

    c. If the mysteries of death were revealed, everyone would be filled with fear.   T ☐ F ☐

    d. If they were revealed, everyone would long for death.   T ☐ F ☐

    e. For the true believer, death is life.   T ☐ F ☐

f. All knowledge of life after death is with God.   T ☐   F ☐

g. Death is the bearer of gladness.   T ☐   F ☐

h. The mysteries of death have been revealed and are
    read by all.   T ☐   F ☐

i. It is important for us to know about life after death.   T ☐   F ☐

2. Fill in the blank spaces:

a. The mysteries of death have not been _____

    _____

b. If they were revealed, they would evoke _____

    _____

    _____

c. Those that have not been firm in the Covenant would feel_____

    _____

d. Those that have been firm in the Covenant would be filled with so much
    _____ that they would _____ for death.

SECTION 5

Bahá'u'lláh says:

> **"The purpose of God in creating man hath been, and will ever be, to enable him to know his Creator and to attain His Presence. To this most excellent aim, this supreme objective, all the heavenly Books and the divinely-revealed and weighty Scriptures unequivocally bear witness. Whoso hath recognized the Day Spring of Divine guidance and entered His holy court hath drawn nigh unto God and attained His Presence, a Presence which is the real Paradise, and of which the loftiest mansions of heaven are but a symbol. . . . Whoso hath failed to recognize Him will have condemned himself to the misery of remoteness, a remoteness which is naught but utter nothingness and the essence of the nethermost fire. Such will be his fate, though to outward seeming he may occupy the earth's loftiest seats and be established upon its most exalted throne."** [3]

1. Questions:

a. What was God's purpose in creating man? _____

    _____

b. Does this purpose change from age to age? _____

c. Which books confirm this purpose? _____
_____

d. Who is the "Day Spring of Divine guidance"? _____

e. To whom are we drawing near when we recognize the "Day Spring of Divine guidance"? _____

f. What is "real Paradise"? _____
_____

g. What can we expect if we do not recognize the "Day Spring of Divine guidance"?
_____

h. What condition do "utter nothingness" and "nethermost fire" refer to? _____
_____
_____

SECTION 6

'Abdu'l-Bahá says:

> **"In the beginning of his human life man was embryonic in the world of the matrix. There he received capacity and endowment for the reality of human existence. The forces and powers necessary for this world were bestowed upon him in that limited condition. In this world he needed eyes; he received them potentially in the other. He needed ears; he obtained them there in readiness and preparation for his new existence. The powers requisite in this world were conferred upon him in the world of the matrix . . .**
>
> **"Therefore, in this world he must prepare himself for the life beyond. That which he needs in the world of the Kingdom must be obtained here. Just as he prepared himself in the world of the matrix by acquiring forces necessary in this sphere of existence, so, likewise, the indispensable forces of the divine existence must be potentially attained in this world."** [4]

1. Mark true or false:

   a. We received the capacities and endowments we need for this world in the world of the matrix.　　T ☐　F ☐

   b. Our condition in the matrix was not limited.　　T ☐　F ☐

c. All forces and powers necessary for this world were bestowed upon us in the world of the matrix. T ☐ F ☐

d. There is no need to prepare oneself for the next life. T ☐ F ☐

e. What we need in the world of the Kingdom can be obtained there. T ☐ F ☐

f. The purpose of this life is to acquire the forces and powers necessary for the next life. T ☐ F ☐

g. True life begins when one dies and goes to the divine Kingdom. T ☐ F ☐

h. True life is the life of the soul. T ☐ F ☐

i. True life begins in this world and continues after physical death. T ☐ F ☐

2. Questions:

a. How does man begin his life? _____
_____

b. Where does he receive his capacities and endowments? _____
_____
_____

c. What are some of the things that man needs in this life that are given to him in the world of the matrix? _____
_____
_____

d. Which endowments should be obtained here for life after death? _____
_____
_____

SECTION 7

Bahá'u'lláh says:

> "The whole duty of man in this Day is to attain that share of the flood of grace which God poureth forth for him. Let none, therefore, consider the largeness or smallness of the receptacle. The portion of some might lie in the palm of a man's hand, the portion of others might fill a cup, and of others even a gallon-measure." [5]

1. Exercises:

   a. Mention some of the blessings you have received from God. _____

   _____

   _____

   b. Give examples of how man keeps himself from receiving his portion of God's grace. _____

   _____

   _____

   c. Why should we not consider "the largeness or smallness" of our receptacle?

   _____

   _____

2. Mark true or false:

   a. Only the great philosophers have the capacity to know God.   T ☐   F ☐

   b. To serve God, we need to forget our weaknesses and trust in Him.   T ☐   F ☐

   c. If in this world we do not develop what God has given us, our souls will be weak when we arrive in the next world.   T ☐   F ☐

SECTION 8

Bahá'u'lláh says:

> **"Thou hast asked Me concerning the nature of the soul. Know, verily, that the soul is a sign of God, a heavenly gem whose reality the most learned of men hath failed to grasp, and whose mystery no mind, however acute, can ever hope to unravel. It is the first among all created things to declare the excellence of its Creator, the first to recognize His glory, to cleave to His truth, and to bow down in adoration before Him. If it be faithful to God, it will reflect His light, and will, eventually, return unto Him. If it fail, however, in its allegiance to its Creator, it will become a victim to self and passion, and will, in the end, sink in their depths."** [6]

1. Fill in the blank spaces:

   a. The soul is a _____ of God.

   b. _____ is a heavenly gem.

   c. _____ is the first to declare the excellence of its Creator.

d. The soul will return to God if it is _____

e. The soul will become a victim of self and passion if _____

_____

f. If it becomes a victim of self, the soul will sink in the depths of _____

_____

g. A soul reflects the light of God if it is _____

_____

2. Mark true or false:

a. "To unravel" means to find out.   T ☐   F ☐

b. Among all created things, the first to recognize God is the mind.   T ☐   F ☐

c. "Acute" means sharp.   T ☐   F ☐

d. A learned person understands the mystery of the soul.   T ☐   F ☐

e. It is not necessary to meditate about the soul because we will never be able to understand it.   T ☐   F ☐

SECTION 9

Bahá'u'lláh says:

> "Ye are even as the bird which soareth, with the full force of its mighty wings and with complete and joyous confidence, through the immensity of the heavens, until, impelled to satisfy its hunger, it turneth longingly to the water and clay of the earth below it, and, having been entrapped in the mesh of its desire, findeth itself impotent to resume its flight to the realms whence it came. Powerless to shake off the burden weighing on its sullied wings, that bird, hitherto an inmate of the heavens, is now forced to seek a dwelling-place upon the dust. Wherefore, O My servants, defile not your wings with the clay of waywardness and vain desires, and suffer them not to be stained with the dust of envy and hate, that ye may not be hindered from soaring in the heavens of My divine knowledge." [7]

1. Fill in the blank spaces:

a. The bird to which Bahá'u'lláh refers in this quotation is the _____ of man.

b. This bird is an inhabitant of the _____

c. This bird is now forced to seek its home in the _____

2. Exercises:

    a. How could the "wings" of the soul become "sullied"? _____

    _____

    b. Describe some burdens that are like "the water and clay of the earth". _____

    _____

    _____

    _____

    c. What is it that can impede us from soaring again in the heaven of divine knowledge?

    _____

    d. Give some examples of things that impede our soaring to the heavens of divine knowledge. _____

    _____

    _____

    e. Why would a soul exchange its heavenly home for the dust of this world? ___

    _____

    _____

SECTION 10

Bahá'u'lláh says:

> **"Having created the world and all that liveth and moveth therein, He, through the direct operation of His unconstrained and sovereign Will, chose to confer upon man the unique distinction and capacity to know Him and to love Him—a capacity that must needs be regarded as the generating impulse and the primary purpose underlying the whole of creation. . . . Upon the inmost reality of each and every created thing He hath shed the light of one of His names, and made it a recipient of the glory of one of His attributes. Upon the reality of man, however, He hath focused the radiance of all of His names and attributes, and made it a mirror of His own Self. Alone of all created things man hath been singled out for so great a favor, so enduring a bounty."** [8]

1. Exercises:

    a. What special distinction has God conferred upon man? _____

    _____

b. Mention some of the attributes of God. _____

_____

_____

c. God has shed upon the reality of each thing the light of one of His _____

_____

d. Upon the reality of man He has focused the radiance of _____

_____ and made it a mirror of _____

e. Mention some of the attributes of God reflected in man's soul. _____

_____

_____

f. How can these attributes be manifested? _____

_____

g. For what special favor has man been singled out? _____

_____

_____

2. Mark true or false in the light of the last two quotations:

a. Worldly attachments impede our spiritual progress. T ☐ F ☐

b. Our passions and desires are not barriers that impede
    our flight towards the Kingdom of God. T ☐ F ☐

c. We can be rid of the burdens that prevent us from
    ascending to God by detaching ourselves from the
    things of this world. T ☐ F ☐

d. The soul's home is the dust. T ☐ F ☐

e. Envy, hatred, and malice are not a burden for the
    soul's progress. T ☐ F ☐

f. Nothing can impede the Will of God. T ☐ F ☐

g. Man is equal to the rest of creation. T ☐ F ☐

h. Knowledge of God is the generating impulse and the
    primary purpose underlying the whole of creation. T ☐ F ☐

i. The reality of every created thing manifests one of
    the attributes of God. T ☐ F ☐

SECTION 11

Bahá'u'lláh says:

> "These energies with which the Day Star of Divine bounty and Source of heavenly guidance hath endowed the reality of man lie, however, latent within him, even as the flame is hidden within the candle and the rays of light are potentially present in the lamp. The radiance of these energies may be obscured by worldly desires even as the light of the sun can be concealed beneath the dust and dross which cover the mirror. Neither the candle nor the lamp can be lighted through their own unaided efforts, nor can it ever be possible for the mirror to free itself from its dross. It is clear and evident that until a fire is kindled the lamp will never be ignited, and unless the dross is blotted out from the face of the mirror it can never represent the image of the sun nor reflect its light and glory." [9]

1. Questions:

    a. What does the word "latent" mean? _____

    _____

    _____

    b. What capacities are latent in the soul of man? _____

    _____

    _____

    _____

    c. What potential does a lamp have? _____

    d. What potential does a mirror have? _____

    e. What do you have to do to a lamp so that it may give light? _____

    _____

    f. What do you have to do to a mirror so it will reflect light? _____

    _____

    g. Can the lamp and the mirror manifest their potentials by themselves? _____

    h. How can we relate these two examples to the condition of the human soul?

    _____

    _____

    _____

i.   Who can make the soul of man manifest its potentials? _____

_____

_____

SECTION 12

Bahá'u'lláh says:

> **"The door of the knowledge of the Ancient Being hath ever been, and will con-tinue for ever to be, closed in the face of men. No man's understanding shall ever gain access unto His holy court. As a token of His mercy, however, and as a proof of His loving-kindness, He hath manifested unto men the Day Stars of His divine guidance, the Symbols of His divine unity, and hath ordained the knowledge of these sanctified Beings to be identical with the knowledge of His own Self. Whoso recognizeth them hath recognized God. Whoso hearkeneth to their call, hath hearkened to the Voice of God, and whoso testifieth to the truth of their Revelation, hath testified to the truth of God Himself. Whoso turneth away from them, hath turned away from God, and whoso disbelieveth in them, hath disbelieved in God. Every one of them is the Way of God that connecteth this world with the realms above, and the Standard of His Truth unto every one in the kingdoms of earth and heaven. They are the Manifestations of God amidst men, the evidences of His Truth, and the signs of His glory."** [10]

1.   Exercises:

a.   We know that only God can cause the soul of man to manifest its capacities, but is it possible for man to know God directly? _____

b.   How, then, can we know God? _____

_____

c.   Name some of the Day Stars of divine guidance. _____

_____

d.   What knowledge is identical with the knowledge of God? _____

_____

e.   What voice have those who have listened to the Manifestations of God hearkened to? _____

f.   Who are we turning away from when we do not heed the call of the Manifesta-tions of God? _____

2. Complete the following phrases:

   a. The door of the knowledge of the Ancient Being hath ever been, and will continue for ever to be _____

   b. No man's understanding shall ever gain access unto _____

   _____

   c. God sent His Manifestations as a token of His _____

   d. The knowledge of the Manifestations of God is identical with _____

   _____

   e. Whoso recognizeth Them has _____

   f. Whoso hearkeneth to Their call has _____

   _____

   g. Every one of Them is the Way of God that _____

   _____

   _____

SECTION 13

Bahá'u'lláh says:

> **"Man is the supreme Talisman. Lack of a proper education hath, however, deprived him of that which he doth inherently possess. Through a word proceeding out of the mouth of God he was called into being; by one word more he was guided to recognize the Source of his education; by yet another word his station and destiny were safeguarded. The Great Being saith: Regard man as a mine rich in gems of inestimable value. Education can, alone, cause it to reveal its treasures, and enable mankind to benefit therefrom. If any man were to meditate on that which the Scriptures, sent down from the heaven of God's holy Will, have revealed, he would readily recognize that their purpose is that all men shall be regarded as one soul, so that the seal bearing the words 'The Kingdom shall be God's' may be stamped on every heart, and the light of Divine bounty, of grace, and mercy may envelop all mankind." [11]**

1. Questions:

   a. What does "talisman" mean? _____

b. What effects have lack of education had on man? _____
_____

c. What can a proper education cause? _____
_____
_____

d. What is the Source of man's education? _____

e. What is man's destiny? _____
_____

f. What are some of the gems education reveals in man? _____
_____

g. What is the purpose of God's Revelation? _____
_____

h. What words will be stamped on the hearts of men? _____
_____

2. Mark true or false:

a. Man will become a spiritual being by his own efforts.   T ☐   F ☐

b. God gave man his mind and it is sufficient for his
progress.   T ☐   F ☐

c. Man will progress spiritually by recognizing the Manifestation of God and will not have to put forth more
effort.   T ☐   F ☐

d. Man can only progress spiritually by recognizing the
Manifestation of God and then by putting forth effort
to live according to His teachings.   T ☐   F ☐

e. Man can directly know God.   T ☐   F ☐

f. Man can become like God.   T ☐   F ☐

g. God is exalted above the comprehension of men.   T ☐   F ☐

h. When we listen to the Words of a Manifestation of
God, we are listening to the Voice of God.   T ☐   F ☐

i. Only through the Manifestations of God is man able
to reflect the attributes of God.   T ☐   F ☐

SECTION 14

Bahá'u'lláh says:

"**Blessed is the soul which, at the hour of its separation from the body, is sanctified from the vain imaginings of the peoples of the world. Such a soul liveth and moveth in accordance with the Will of its Creator, and entereth the all-highest Paradise. The Maids of Heaven, inmates of the loftiest mansions, will circle around it, and the Prophets of God and His chosen ones will seek its companionship. With them that soul will freely converse, and will recount unto them that which it hath been made to endure in the path of God, the Lord of all worlds.**" [12]

"**The souls of the infidels, however, shall—and to this I bear witness—when breathing their last be made aware of the good things that have escaped them, and shall bemoan their plight, and shall humble themselves before God. They shall continue doing so after the separation of their souls from their bodies.**" [13]

"**He should forgive the sinful, and never despise his low estate, for none knoweth what his own end shall be. How often hath a sinner attained, at the hour of death, to the essence of faith, and, quaffing the immortal draught, hath taken his flight unto the Concourse on high! And how often hath a devout believer, at the hour of his soul's ascension, been so changed as to fall into the nethermost fire!**" [14]

1. Questions:

    a. What should the condition of our soul be when it separates from the body? __
    _____

    b. What are some vain imaginings? _____
    _____
    _____
    _____

    c. Where do the souls sanctified from vain imaginings go? _____
    _____
    _____

    d. With whom will these souls find themselves? _____
    _____

    e. Will these souls be able to converse with the Prophets of God? _____

    f. Does this position seem great? Do you want to attain it? _____

g. Who are the infidels? _____

_____

h. What do the souls of the unbelievers recognize when breathing their last breath?

_____

i. What will they do once they recognize their condition? _____

_____

_____

j. Do we know beforehand how and when our life will end? _____

k. What can we do now to assure our eternal life? _____

_____

_____

l. What spiritual qualities do we associate with attaining eternal life? _____

_____

_____

SECTION 15

'Abdu'l-Bahá says:

> "The mysteries of which man is heedless in this earthly world, those will he discover in the heavenly world, and there will he be informed of the secret of truth; how much more will he recognize or discover persons with whom he hath been associated. Undoubtedly, the holy souls who find a pure eye and are favored with insight will, in the kingdom of lights, be acquainted with all mysteries, and will seek the bounty of witnessing the reality of every great soul. Even they will manifestly behold the Beauty of God in that world. Likewise will they find all the friends of God, both those of the former and recent times, present in the heavenly assemblage." [15]

> "The difference and distinction will naturally become realized between all men after their departure from this mortal world. But this (distinction) is not in respect to place, but it is in respect to the soul and conscience. For the Kingdom of God is sanctified (or free) from time and place; it is another world and another universe. But the holy souls are promised the gift of intercession. And know thou for a certainty, that in the divine worlds, the spiritual beloved ones (believers) will recognize each other, and will seek union (with each other), but a spiritual union. Likewise, a love that one may have entertained for any one will not be forgotten in the world of the Kingdom. Likewise, thou wilt not forget (there) the life that thou hast had in the material world." [16]

1.　Questions:

　　　a.　What mysteries will man discover in the heavenly world? _____

　　　　　_____

　　　　　_____

　　　b.　Will we recognize people we have known in this world? _____

　　　c.　Which souls will be acquainted with all mysteries? _____

　　　　　_____

　　　d.　Will there be differences and distinctions among the souls? _____

　　　　　_____

　　　e.　From what is the Kingdom of God free? _____

　　　　　_____

　　　f.　What will remain of the bonds of love that unite two people in this world? __

　　　　　_____

2.　Mark true or false:

　　　a.　Souls will not recognize one another in the heavenly
　　　　　world.　　　　　　　　　　　　　　　　　　　　T ☐　　F ☐

　　　b.　The holy souls will seek the grace of the presence of
　　　　　every great soul.　　　　　　　　　　　　　　　T ☐　　F ☐

　　　c.　The celestial concourse includes pure souls of past
　　　　　times.　　　　　　　　　　　　　　　　　　　　T ☐　　F ☐

　　　d.　Naturally, differences and distinctions will not mani-
　　　　　fest themselves after the souls leave this world.　　T ☐　　F ☐

　　　e.　The Kingdom of God is free from time and space.　　T ☐　　F ☐

　　　f.　The other world pertains to another universe.　　　T ☐　　F ☐

　　　g.　In the other world one will forget the love one has
　　　　　had for another person.　　　　　　　　　　　　T ☐　　F ☐

SECTION 16

Bahá'u'lláh says:

> "Thou hast, moreover, asked Me concerning the state of the soul after its separation from the body. Know thou, of a truth, that if the soul of man hath walked in the ways of God, it will, assuredly, return and be gathered to the glory of the Beloved. By the righteousness of God! It shall attain a station such as no pen can depict, or tongue describe. The soul that hath remained faithful to the Cause of God, and stood unwaveringly firm in His Path shall, after his ascension, be possessed of such power that all the worlds which the Almighty hath created can benefit through him." [17]

1. Complete the following phrases:

    a. If the soul of man has walked in the ways of God, it will, assuredly _____

    _____

    _____

    b. It will attain a station such as _____

    _____

    c. The _____ that has remained _____ to the

    _____ of _____, and has _____ unwaveringly

    _____ in _____ shall, after _____

    _____, be possessed of such _____ that all the

    worlds which the _____ hath _____

    can _____ through him.

SECTION 17

Bahá'u'lláh says:

> "O My servants! Sorrow not if, in these days and on this earthly plane, things contrary to your wishes have been ordained and manifested by God, for days of blissful joy, of heavenly delight, are assuredly in store for you. Worlds, holy and spiritually glorious, will be unveiled to your eyes. You are destined by Him, in this world and hereafter, to partake of their benefits, to share in their joys, and to obtain a portion of their sustaining grace. To each and every one of them you will, no doubt, attain." [18]

1. Mark true or false:

    a. We should be sad when things are not the way we
        want them to be.   T ☐   F ☐

b. All, be it good or bad, is ordained by God.   T ☐   F ☐

c. We are assured of days of happiness.   T ☐   F ☐

d. The other worlds of God are holy and spiritually glorious.   T ☐   F ☐

e. It is our destiny to partake of the benefits of these worlds, in this life and the life hereafter.   T ☐   F ☐

2. Complete the following phrases:

a. We should not _____ if things contrary to our wishes occur.

b. Days of _____ and _____ are in store for us.

c. We will see worlds _____ and _____

d. God assures us a portion of their sustaining grace in _____ world and _____

e. In these worlds, we will partake of their _____, share in their _____, and obtain a portion of their _____

3. Questions:

a. Why should we not be saddened when things contrary to our wishes occur?

_____

_____

b. What is the promise Bahá'u'lláh makes to us in this passage? _____

_____

SECTION 18

In this course, you have studied and meditated on the true meaning of human life. You have learned from different quotations of Bahá'u'lláh and 'Abdu'l-Bahá a great deal about the nature of the soul, the purpose of life, and the need for developing spiritual qualities in this world, and about the promises of an eternal life, full of joy and glory, for those who have recognized the Manifestation of God and remained steadfast in His love. It would be appropriate for you to end this course by thinking about the effect this new understanding will have on your life. How will you live now, knowing as you do, that your earthly life is but a small part of a life that is eternal, a life for which you must prepare purposefully and perseveringly?

To help you think about the decisions you will have to make in your life, a few themes, each of which could be the subject of hours and hours of meditation, are mentioned here. You may like to write a few paragraphs about each theme, or discuss them with a small group of your friends.

Now that I understand that my life begins here on earth but leads me towards God for all eternity, how important are the following aspects of my life for me?

1. *Obedience to the laws of Bahá'u'lláh*
2. *My contribution to the well-being of the human race*
3. *My service to the Cause and to humanity*
4. *My firmness in the Covenant*

REFERENCES

1. *Gleanings from the Writings of Bahá'u'lláh* (Wilmette: Bahá'í Publishing Trust, 1994), LXXXI, pp. 155-56.

2. Ibid., CLXV, pp. 345-46.

3. Ibid., XXIX, pp. 70-71.

4. *The Promulgation of Universal Peace: Talks Delivered by 'Abdu'l-Bahá during His Visit to the United States and Canada in 1912* (Wilmette: Bahá'í Publishing Trust, 1995), pp. 225-26.

5. *Gleanings from the Writings of Bahá'u'lláh*, V, p. 8.

6. Ibid., LXXXII, pp. 158-59.

7. Ibid., CLIII, p. 327.

8. Ibid., XXVII, p. 65.

9. Ibid., XXVII, pp. 65-66.

10. Ibid., XXI, pp. 49-50.

11. Ibid., CXXII, pp. 259-60.

12. Ibid., LXXXI, p. 156.

13. Ibid., LXXXVI, pp. 170-71.

14. Ibid., CXXV, p. 266.

15. *Tablets of Abdul-Baha Abbas* (New York: Bahá'í Publishing Committee, 1930), vol. 1, p. 205.

16. Ibid., pp. 205-6.

17. *Gleanings from the Writings of Bahá'u'lláh,* LXXXII, p. 161.

18. Ibid., CLIII, p. 329.